CB126813

With digital materials

digital Including additional Festival lessons (**Halloween, Christmas, Carnival**)

macmillan education

Sandie Mourão

Course consultant: Claire Medwell

Macmillan Education
4 Crinan Street
London N1 9XW
A division of Macmillan Publishers Limited

Companies and representatives throughout the world

Pupil's Book PLUS ISBN 978-0-230-44662-5

First published 2015

Original design by Anthony Godber
Page make-up by Carolyn Gibson
Original character concept by Mike Brownlow
Illustrated by Pablo Gallego (Beehive Illustration)
Additional artwork provided by Leo Brown, Tamara Joubert, Martyn Cain, Fran Brylewski, David Brylewski, Nathalie Ortega Garcia (Beehive Illustration)
Cover design by Macmillan Publishers Limited and Astwood Design Consultancy
Cover illustration by Pablo Gallego (Beehive Illustration)
Picture research by Emily Taylor

Authors' acknowledgements:
Many thanks to the Macmillan team. Special thanks to Claire Medwell.

The publishers would like to thank:
Ana Belén Alonso Lucas, CEIP Miguel Hernández, Jumilla, Murcia; Ana Demitro, English Studio, Narón, A Coruña; Celia Mercader Rodríguez, CEIP Sta. María de Gracia, Murcia; Christine Brook, Col·legi Alzines, Girona; Cristina Lión Jornet, CEIP Alhambra, Madrid; Eva Almagro Caballero, CEIP Joaquín Blume, Torrejón de Ardoz, Madrid; Fabiola Cintrón Dapena, EEI Concepción Crespo Rivas, Pontevedra; Irene Cristòfol Mora, Escola Pompeu Fabra, Vilanova i la Gertrú, Barcelona; Isabel Mangas Álvarez, CEIP Francisco Fatou, Madrid; Isabel Melcón Pérez, Madrid; Julie Hickin, Sant Cugat del Vallès, Barcelona; Mª Rosa Medina Marín, CEIP Francisco Giner de los Ríos, Murcia; Mª Jesús Pérez González, CEIP Camilo José Cela, Madrid; Mª del Puy Salas Fernández, Colegio María Auxiliadora, Madrid; Mercedes Peinado Sánchez, CEIP Dr. Conde de Arruga, Madrid; Mercedes Zarza García, CEIP Tirso de Molina, Madrid; Miren Begoña Ugarte Urrejola, CEIP Kanpazar HLHI, Portugalete, Vizcaya; Mónica Vicente García, CEIP Pinar del Rey, Madrid; Nieves Fernández Reche, Colegio Inmaculada Niña, Granada; Noemí Navas Arranz, Escola Bufalà, Badalona, Barcelona; Paloma Radillo Cruz, CEIP María Moliner, Madrid; Philippa Hirst, Colegio Internacional Ausiàs March, Picassent, Valencia; Yvonne Dalorto, Laude Altillo School, Jerez de la Frontera, Cádiz.

Printed in Brazil by Forma Certa

2022
16

The authors and publishers would like to thank the following for permission to reproduce their photographs:

Alamy/Juniors Bildarchiv p83(tr), Alamy/Larry Lilac p71(tl), Alamy/Trevor Pearson p71(bl), Alamy/Rafal Stachura p71(tcl); **Bridgeman Art Library**/Harlequin, 1890 (oil on canvas), Cezanne, Paul (1839-1906)/Private Collection/Photo © Lefevre Fine Art Ltd., London/The Bridgeman Art Library p115(1 – image on poster); **Fergus Burnett** pp 11, 18, 23, 30, 35, 42, 47, 54, 59(tl, bl), 66, 78, 90, 102, 113, 117; **Corbis**/Thomas Kremer/The Food Passionates p71(tml), Corbis/Tim Mitchell/Arcaid p59(tr); **Getty Images**/Dorling Kindersley p71(cml), Getty Images/LWA p83(br), Getty Images/Vetta pp10, 22, 34, 46, 58, 70, 82, 94; Getty Images/Brooke Slezak pp13, 25, 37, 49, 61, 73, 85, 97; **Superstock** p83(tl); **ThinkStock**/Getty Images/iStockphoto pp59(br), 71(cl, bcl, bcml, bml), 83(bl), ThinkStock/Zoonar p71(bml).

Commissioned photographs by **Fergus Burnett** pp 11, 18, 23, 30, 35, 42, 47, 54, 59 (tl, bl), 66, 78, 90, 102, 113, 117.

The authors and publishers are grateful for permission to reprint the following copyright material:

'If You're Happy and You Know It (Clap Your Hands)' from 'Captain Jack Level 0 Multimedia Pack' © J. Leighton; S. Mourao 2012, Published by Macmillan Publishers Limited. Used by Permission. All Rights Reserved.

'Baa Baa Black Sheep' from 'Captain Jack Level 1 Multimedia Pack' © J. Leighton 2012, Published by Macmillan Publishers Limited. Used by Permission. All Rights Reserved.

'Teddy Bear, Teddy Bear' from 'Captain Jack Level 0 Multimedia Pack' © J. Leighton; S. Mourao 2012, Published by Macmillan Publishers Limited. Used by Permission. All Rights Reserved.

'Boys and Girls Come Out to Play' from 'Captain Jack Level 1 Multimedia Pack' © J. Leighton 2012, Published by Macmillan Publishers Limited. Used by Permission. All Rights Reserved.

The authors and publishers wish to thank the following for their help with the photoshoot: Ann Tayler Children's Centre.

Hello Dex

Vocabulary lesson

Hello Dex

Name: ______________________________

1: Vocabulary lesson

Pupil's Book worksheet *page 3*

CD1 12 **Colours song**

Red, red, yellow and orange
Brown, green and blue

Red, red, yellow and orange
Brown, green and blue

Tickle my tummy
Tickle my tummy
Tickle my tummy, oh, oh, oh, oh

- Point to the characters in the picture and say their names.
- Trace Dex.
- Colour Dex's spots red, yellow, orange, brown, green and blue.
- Point and say the colours on Dex's tummy.
- Sing *Colours* and point to the colours.

Personalisation Discover for yourself

Extra activity Draw a picture of Meg and Charlie. Use red, yellow, orange, brown, green and blue crayons.

Hello Dex

Vocabulary lesson

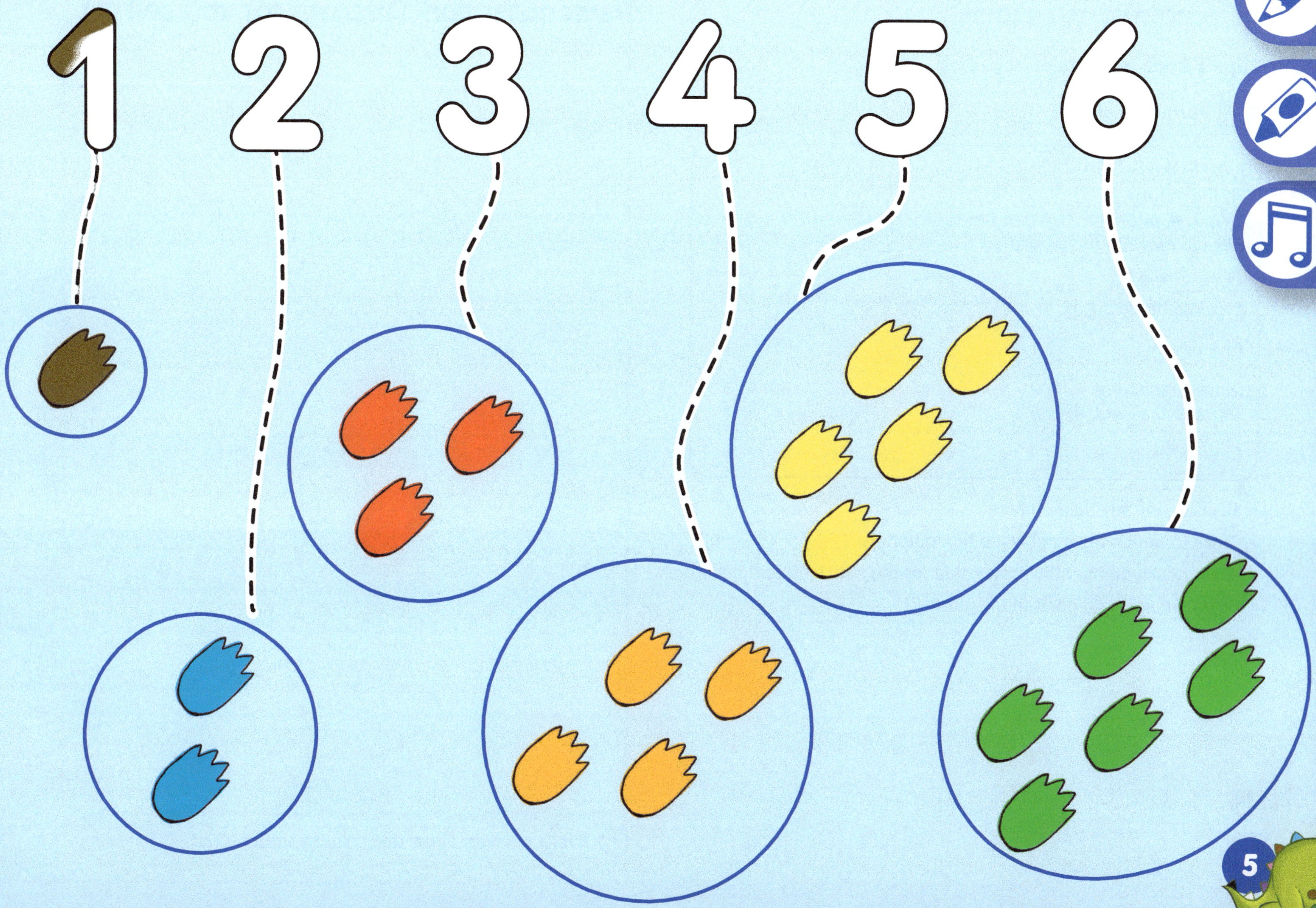

Hello Dex

Name: ______________________

2: Vocabulary lesson

Pupil's Book worksheet *page 5*

CD1 13 **Numbers song**

I like to move (x3)
To the groove
1, 2, 3, 4, 5, 6
I like to move to the groove

Move to the left, 1, 2, 3
Move to the left, 4, 5, 6

Chorus

Move to the right, 1, 2, 3
Move to the right, 4, 5, 6

Chorus

- Point to and say the numbers.
- Trace to match the numbers to the footprints.
- Colour each number the same colour as the matching footprints.
- Sing *Numbers* and point to the numbers.

Personalisation Discover for yourself

Extra activity Draw and colour your footprints.

1 Discover my classroom

Vocabulary lesson

1 Discover my classroom

Name: ____________________

1: Vocabulary lesson

Pupil's Book worksheet *page 7*

CD1 16 CD1 17 **My Classroom song**

Hello, hello, hello
Welcome to my classroom!
Hello, hello, hello
Welcome to my school!
(x2)

Can you see a table? Yes, I can!
Can you see a chair? Yes, I can!
Can you see a pencil? Yes, I can!

Chorus

Can you see a crayon? Yes, I can!
Can you see a book? Yes, I can!
Can you see a sticker? Yes, I can!

Chorus

- Point to the classroom objects and say the words.
- Trace and colour the magnified pictures.
- Match the classroom objects to the magnified pictures.
- Colour the magnified pictures to match.
- Circle the classroom objects that have not been magnified.
- Sing *My Classroom* and point to the classroom objects.

digital **Teacher's Presentation Kit for Unit 1**

Personalisation Discover for yourself

Extra activity Draw your classroom.

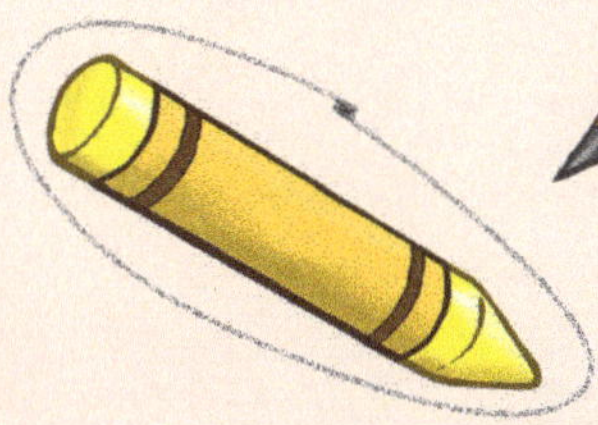

1 Discover my classroom

Name: ____________________

2: Story lesson

Pupil's Book worksheet *page 9*

CD1 18 **Have You Got A Sticker? story**

Classroom behaviour

- Point to the classroom objects and say the words.
- Circle the objects you need to complete the picture.
- Trace and colour the tree and colour the picture.

3: Concepts lesson

Photocopiable worksheet *Teacher's Book page 174*

CD1 19 CD1 20 **How Are You Today? song**

Hello, how are you? (x2)
How are you today?

I'm sad! Boo hoo!
I'm sad today

Chorus

I'm happy! Ha ha ha ha ha! (x2)
I'm happy today!

Chorus

I'm surprised! Oh! (x2)
I'm surprised today!

- Point to the characters and say their names.
- Point and say *happy*, *sad* or *surprised*.
- Circle the matching emotions in each row.
- Colour each emotion a different colour and say the colours and emotions.
- Sing *How Are You Today?* and point to the emotions.

Dex's values lesson

Classroom behaviour

1 Discover my classroom

Name: ______________________________

4: Buddy's sounds lesson

Photocopiable worksheet *Teacher's Book page 175*

CD1 21 **Buddy's Beats rap /b/**

1, 2, 3, say with me
/b/, /b/, /b/
/b/ Buddy!

1, 2, 3, say with me
/b/, /b/, /b/
/b/ brown!

1, 2, 3, say with me
/b/, /b/, /b/
/b/ blue!

1, 2, 3, say with me
/b/, /b/, /b/
/b/ book!

- Trace the letter /b/.
- Say the sound.
- Point to the pictures and say the words.
- Colour the words beginning with /b/.
- Say *Buddy's Beats* and point to the words beginning with /b/.

5: Dex's values lesson: Classroom behaviour

Pupil's Book worksheet *page 11*

- Point to the photos and say *listen carefully, hands up* or *tidy up*.
- Trace the tick for good behaviour and the cross for bad behaviour.
- Draw a happy face on the teacher if the photo shows good behaviour.
- Draw a sad face on the teacher if the photo shows bad behaviour.
- Point to the teacher and say *happy* or *sad*.

1 Discover my classroom

Name: ______________________

6: Kid's culture lesson

Pupil's Book worksheet *page 13*

CD1 22 CD1 23 **If You're Happy, Happy, Happy nursery rhyme**

If you're happy, happy, happy, clap your hands (x2)
If you're happy, happy, happy, clap your hands

If you're happy, happy, happy, wave your arms (x2)
If you're happy, happy, happy, wave your arms

If you're happy, happy, happy, turn around (x2)
If you're happy, happy, happy, turn around

If you're happy, happy, happy, say 'Hooray!' (x2)
If you're happy, happy, happy, say 'Hooray!'

- Point to the pictures and say *happy*.
- Trace the frames.
- Draw yourself feeling happy.
- Sing *If You're Happy, Happy, Happy* and point to the pictures.

7: Speaking and literacy lesson

CD1 18 **Pupil's Book worksheet (storybook)** *pages 15–16*

- Cut out and fold the pages to make the storybook.
- Listen to the story and follow the storybook with your finger.

8: Review lesson

Pupil's Book worksheet *page 17*

- Go to the sticker pages. Complete the picture with the unit stickers.
- Point to the classroom objects and say the words.
- Stick Dex's star in the correct place.

Pupil's Book worksheet *page 18*

- Point to the pictures and say the activities.
- Draw a happy/sad face if you can/can't do the activity.

9: PLUS vocabulary lesson / Extension

Photocopiable worksheet *Teacher's Book page 176*

CD1 27 CD1 28 **My Classroom PLUS song**

- Point to and say the classroom objects.
- Trace.
- Match the classroom objects.
- Colour each object a different colour and say the colours.
- Sing *My Classroom PLUS* and point to the classroom objects.

MY STORYBOOK

Name: ______________________

1 Have You Got a Sticker?

5

2

1
HELPER
TODAY
TODAY IS...
MONTH DAY
DAY
DATE
MONTH
YEAR
WEATHER
SEASON
SEASON
WEATHER
HELPER
6
HELPER
3
4
HELPER

Unit 1 review lesson

My learning review

My progress review

Name: ____________________

I can …

Teacher: ____________________ Comments: ____________________

Halloween

Lesson 1

Halloween

Name: ____________________

Lesson 1

Pupil's Book worksheet *page 19*

- Match each scene to the character who is missing. (There is one character missing from each scene.)
- Circle the character who appears in all the pictures.

digital **Teacher's Resource Centre for Halloween Lesson 2, Christmas lessons and Carnival lessons**

Personalisation Discover for yourself

Extra activity: Draw your favourite Halloween costume.

2 Discover toys
Vocabulary lesson

2 Discover toys

Name: ______________________

1: Vocabulary lesson

Pupil's Book worksheet *page 21*

CD1 30 CD1 31 **Come And Play song**

Come and play with my car (x2)

Come and play with my scooter (x2)

Come and play with my ball (x2)

Come and play with my doll (x2)

Come and play with my computer game (x2)

Come and play with my blocks (x2)

Come and play! (x4)

- Point to the puzzles and say the words.
- Match the puzzles to the correct puzzle pieces.
- Colour the puzzle pieces to match the puzzles.
- Cross out the extra puzzle pieces and say the words.
- Sing *Come And Play* and point to the toys.

digital **Teacher's Presentation Kit for Unit 2**

Personalisation Discover for yourself

Extra activity Draw your favourite toy.

2 Discover toys

Name: ____________________

2: Story lesson

Pupil's Book worksheet *page 23*

CD1 32 **Let's Play Together! story**

- Find the toys in the picture and say the words.
- Colour the toys in the picture.
- Match the characters to the toys they like in the story.

3: Concepts lesson

Photocopiable worksheet *Teacher's Book page 177*

CD1 33 CD1 34 **My Feelings song**

Oooh, it's dark! (x2)
Mum! I'm scared (x2)
Nothing to be scared of (x2)
Alright now! (x2)

I am angry (x2)
Grrr, that's mine (x2)
Let's be kind and share now (x2)
All friends now (x2)

Ahh, it's bed time (x2)
Let's calm down (x2)
Time to go to sleep now (x2)
Tucked up tight, say goodnight
(Goodnight!)

- Point to the emotions and say the words.
- Match an emotion to each character.
- Trace the frame around the picture showing *calm*.
- Colour the pictures.
- Sing *My Feelings* and point to the pictures.

Dex's values lesson

Co-operating

2 Discover toys

Name: ______________________________

4: Buddy's sounds lesson

Photocopiable worksheet *Teacher's Book page 178*

CD1 35 **Buddy's Beats rap /c/**

1, 2, 3, say with me
/c/, /c/, /c/
/c/ car!

1, 2, 3, say with me
/c/, /c/, /c/
/c/ crayon!

1, 2, 3, say with me
/c/, /c/, /c/
/c/ computer game!

1, 2, 3, say with me
/c/, /c/, /c/
/c/ calm!

- Trace the letter /c/.
- Say the sound.
- Point to the pictures and say the words.
- Colour the words beginning with /c/.
- Say *Buddy's Beats* and point to the words beginning with /c/.

5: Dex's values lesson: Co-operating

Pupil's Book worksheet *page 25*

- Point to the photos and say *co-operating* or *not co-operating*.
- Colour green the frame of the photo that shows the children co-operating.
- Match the photo of the children co-operating to the completed tower block.

Kid's culture lesson

2 Discover toys

Name: ______________________

6: Kid's culture lesson

Pupil's Book worksheet *page 27*

CD1 36 CD1 37 **Teddy Bear, Teddy Bear nursery rhyme**

Teddy bear, teddy bear, turn around
Teddy bear, teddy bear, touch the ground
Teddy bear, teddy bear, touch your toes
Teddy bear, teddy bear, wiggle your nose

Teddy bear, teddy bear, nod your head
Teddy bear, teddy bear, go to bed
Teddy bear, teddy bear, close your eyes
Teddy bear, teddy bear, say 'Good night'

- Look at the pictures. Colour the spot green if you can do the action and red if you cannot.
- Circle your favourite actions.
- Sing *Teddy Bear, Teddy Bear* and point to the pictures.

7: Speaking and literacy lesson

CD1 32 **Pupil's Book worksheet (storybook)** *pages 29–30*

- Cut out and fold the pages to make the storybook.
- Listen to the story and follow the storybook with your finger.

8: Review lesson

Pupil's Book worksheet *page 31*

- Go to the sticker pages. Complete the picture with the unit stickers.
- Point to the toys and say the words.
- Stick Dex's star in the correct place.

Pupil's Book worksheet *page 32*

- Point to the pictures and say the activities.
- Draw a happy/sad face if you can/can't do the activity.

9: PLUS vocabulary lesson / Extension

Photocopiable worksheet *Teacher's Book page 179*

CD1 41 CD1 42 **Come And Play! PLUS song**

- Point to the toys and say the words.
- Draw the missing toy to complete each sequence.
- Colour each type of toy a different colour and say the colours.
- Sing *Come and Play! PLUS* and point to the toys.

MY STORYBOOK

Name: ______________________________

2 Let's Play Together!

5

2

1
6
3
4

My progress review

Name: ______________________

I can …

Teacher: ______________________ **Comments:** ______________________

3 Discover my body

Vocabulary lesson

3 Discover my body

Name: ______________________________

1: Vocabulary lesson

Pupil's Book worksheet *page 33*

CD2 2 CD2 3 **Let's Move! song**

Nod your head (x3) *That's very good!*	*Rub your tummy* (x3) *That's very good!*
Shake your legs (x3) *That's very good!*	*Flap your arms* (x3) *That's very good!*
Stamp your feet (x3) *That's very good!*	*Wave your hands* (x3) *That's very good!*

- Point to Dex's body parts and say the words.
- Trace and colour the body parts to complete the picture.
- Match Dex's body parts to Meg's body parts.
- Sing *Let's Move!* and point to the body parts.

digital **Teacher's Presentation Kit for Unit 3**

Personalisation Discover for yourself

Extra activity Look at Meg and Dex on page 33. Draw a picture of you in the same way.

3 Discover my body

Name: ______________________________

2: Story lesson

Pupil's Book worksheet *page 35*

CD2 4 **Can You Skip? story**

- Point to the actions and say the words.
- Match Dex to the action he can do in the story.
- Circle if you can do the actions.
- Colour Dex.

3: Concepts lesson

Photocopiable worksheet *Teacher's Book page 180*

CD2 5 CD2 6 **Big Or Small song**

Big or small? Big or small?
Can you tell which one it is?
Big or small? Big or small?
I bet you can guess them all!

Daddy's feet are very big
Baby's feet are very small
Dex's head is very big
Buddy's head is very small

Dex's tummy is very big
Charlie's tummy is very small
Mummy's hands are very big
Meg's hands are very small

Big or small? Big or small?
Can you tell which one it is?
Big or small? Big or small?
I bet you can guess them all!

- Point to the body parts and say the words.
- Point again and say *big* or *small*.
- Match the big and small body parts.
- Colour the frames around the big body parts green and the frames around the small body parts orange.
- Sing *Big Or Small* and point to the big and small body parts.

Dex's values lesson

Being active

Name: ______________________________

4: Buddy's sounds lesson

Photocopiable worksheet *Teacher's Book page 181*

CD2 7 **Buddy's Beats rap /h/**

1, 2, 3, say with me
/h/, /h/, /h/
/h/ head!

1, 2, 3 say with me
/h/, /h/, /h/
/h/ hands!

1, 2, 3, say with me
/h/, /h/, /h/
/h/ happy!

- Trace the letter /h/.
- Say the sound.
- Point to the pictures and say the words.
- Colour the words beginning with /h/.
- Say *Buddy's Beats* and point to the words beginning with /h/.

5: Dex's values lesson: Being active

Pupil's Book worksheet *page 37*

- Look at the photos and say if the activity is *active* or *not active*.
- Trace the tick if the photo shows being active.
- Trace the cross if the photo doesn't show being active.
- Colour the frames if you can do the activity.

3 Discover my body

Name: ______________________________

6: Kid's culture lesson

Pupil's Book worksheet *page 39*

CD2 8 CD2 9 **Head, Shoulders, Knees And Toes nursery rhyme**

Head, shoulders, knees and toes, knees and toes (x2)
And eyes and ears and mouth and nose
Head, shoulders, knees and toes, knees and toes

- Point to the body parts in the pictures and say the words.
- Find and circle the six differences in the bottom picture.
- Trace the tick for the picture that illustrates the nursery rhyme and trace the cross for the picture that doesn't.
- Sing *Head, Shoulders, Knees And Toes* and point to the top picture.

Six differences:
1 the car 2 number three 3 orange t-shirt
4 two pencils 5 touching tummy 6 weather chart

7: Speaking and literacy lesson

CD2 4 **Pupil's Book worksheet (storybook)** *pages 41–42*

- Cut out and fold the pages to make the storybook.
- Listen to the story and follow the storybook with your finger.

8: Review lesson

Pupil's Book worksheet *page 43*

- Go to the sticker pages. Complete the picture with the unit stickers.
- Point to the body parts and say the words.
- Stick Dex's star in the correct place.

Pupil's Book worksheet *page 44*

- Point to the pictures and say the activities.
- Draw a happy/sad face if you can/can't do the activity.

9: PLUS vocabulary lesson / Extension

Photocopiable worksheet *Teacher's Book page 182*

CD2 13 CD2 14 **Let's Move! PLUS song**

- Point to the body parts and say the words.
- Circle the body parts.
- Match Charlie to his shadows.
- Colour the shadows.
- Sing *Let's Move! PLUS* and point to the body parts.

MY STORYBOOK

Name: ____________________

3

Can You Skip?

5

2

1
6
3
4

Unit 3 review lesson

My learning review

Name: ____________________

I can ...

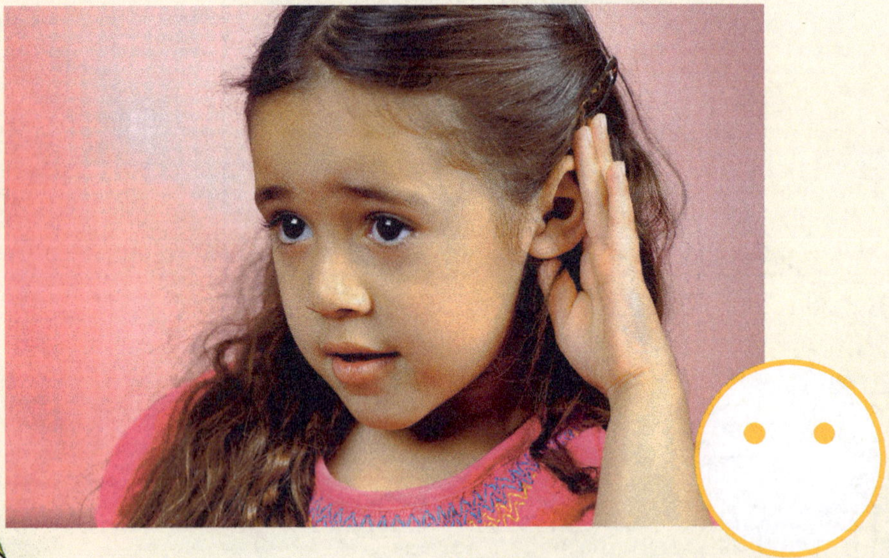

Teacher: ____________________ Comments: ____________________

4 Discover clothes

Vocabulary lesson

4 Discover clothes

Name: ______________________

1: Vocabulary lesson

Pupil's Book worksheet *page 45*

CD2 16 CD2 17 **Let's Get Ready! song**

It's cold, it's cold, brrr!

Put on your T-shirt!
Where's my T-shirt?
It's here! Thank you!

Put on your trousers!
Where are my trousers?
They're here! Thank you!

Put on your socks!
Where are my socks?
They're here! Thank you!

Put on your shoes!
Where are my shoes?
They're here! Thank you!

Put on your coat!
Where's my coat?
It's here! Thank you!

Put on your hat!
Where's my hat?
It's here! Thank you!

- Point to the clothes and say the words.
- Circle the clothes in the picture.
- Colour each piece of clothing to match the clothes in the picture.
- Sing *Let's Get Ready!* and point to the clothes.

digital **Teacher's Presentation Kit for Unit 4**

Personalisation Discover for yourself

Extra activity Draw your favourite clothes.

4 Discover clothes

Name: ______________________________

2: Story lesson

Pupil's Book worksheet *page 47*

CD2 18 **What Am I? story**

- Point to the clothes and say the words.
- Match Meg, Charlie and Dex to the clothes they wear in the story.
- Trace and colour the clothes.

3: Concepts lesson

Photocopiable worksheet *Teacher's Book page 183*

CD2 19 CD2 20 **Shapes song**

A circle, a circle, can you make a circle?
A circle, a circle, I can make a circle! (x2)
Round and round, round and round – look at me!

A square, a square, can you make a square?
A square, a square, I can make a square! (x2)
Four corners, four corners – look at me!

A triangle, a triangle, can you make a triangle?
A triangle, a triangle, I can make a triangle! (x2)
Three corners, three corners – look at me!

- Point to the shapes and say the words.
- Colour the *circles* red, the *triangles* yellow and the *squares* blue.
- Count each shape and circle the correct number.
- Sing *Shapes* and point to the shapes.

4 Discover clothes

Name: ______________________________

4: Buddy's sounds lesson

Photocopiable worksheet *Teacher's Book page 184*

CD2 21 **Buddy's Beats rap /t/**

1, 2, 3, say with me
/t/, /t/, /t/
/t/ table!

1, 2, 3, say with me
/t/, /t/, /t/
/t/ trousers!

1, 2, 3, say with me
/t/, /t/, /t/
/t/ triangle!

1, 2, 3, say with me
/t/, /t/, /t/
/t/ tummy!

- Trace the letter /t/.
- Say the sound.
- Point to the pictures and say the words.
- Colour the words beginning with /t/.
- Say *Buddy's Beats* and point to the words beginning with /t/.

5: Dex's values lesson: Being independent

Pupil's Book worksheet *page 49*

- Look at the photos. Can you do the action? Say *yes* or *no*.
- Match the photos of the girl getting dressed to the correct photos showing the complete outfits.
- Colour the frame around the photos showing your favourite outfit.

Kid's culture lesson

4 Discover clothes

Name: ______________________________

6: Kid's culture lesson

Pupil's Book worksheet *page 51*

CD2 22 CD2 23 **Boys And Girls Come Out To Play nursery rhyme**

Boys and girls come out to play
Put on your coats, it's cold today
Here's a scooter, let's make some noise
And play with all our favourite toys!

- Look at the pictures and say the words.
- Circle the objects mentioned in the nursery rhyme.
- Trace the frame.
- Sing *Boys And Girls Come Out To Play* and point to the pictures.

7: Speaking and literacy lesson

CD2 18 **Pupil's Book worksheet (storybook)** *pages 53–54*

- Cut out and fold the pages to make the storybook.
- Listen to the story and follow the storybook with your finger.

8: Review lesson

Pupil's Book worksheet *page 55*

- Go to the sticker pages. Complete the picture with the unit stickers.
- Point to the clothes and say the words.
- Stick Dex's star in the correct place.

Pupil's Book worksheet *page 56*

- Point to the pictures and say the activities.
- Draw a happy/sad face if you can/can't do the activity.

9: PLUS vocabulary lesson / Extension

Photocopiable worksheet *Teacher's Book page 185*

CD2 27 CD2 28 **Let's Get Ready! PLUS song**

- Point to the clothes and say the words.
- Circle the item of clothing that matches in each row.
- Colour the matching clothes the same colour.
- Sing *Let's Get Ready! PLUS* and point to the clothes.

MY STORYBOOK

Name: ______________________

4

What Am I?

5

2

1
6
3
4

Unit 4 review lesson

My learning review

My progress review

Name: ____________________

I can …

Teacher: ____________________ Comments: ____________________

5 Discover my family

Vocabulary lesson

1

2

1 2 3 4 5 6

5 Discover my family

Name: ______________________

1: Vocabulary lesson

Pupil's Book worksheet *page 57*

CD2 30 CD2 31 **My Family song**

Meet my family! (Happy family!)
Here's my daddy (Happy family!)
Here's my mummy (Happy family!)
My little sister (Happy, happy family!)
My brother and me!
My granny, my grandad!
This is my family (Happy family!)
We all have fun together! (Happy, happy family!)

- Point to the family members and say the words.
- Find and circle the differences in picture 2.
- Circle the number of differences you find.
- Sing *My Family* and point to the family members.

digital **Teacher's Presentation Kit for Unit 5**

Six differences:
1 grandad 2 mummy 3 granny 4 daddy
5 meg's t-shirt 6 charlie's car

Personalisation Discover for yourself

Extra activity Draw your family and friends.

5 Discover my family

Name: ______________________________

2: Story lesson

Pupil's Book Plus worksheet *page 59*

CD2 32 **Let's Tidy Up! story**

- Point to the family members and say the words.
- Match the family members to the objects they ask Dex to put away in the story.
- Draw the missing object in the trolley.
- Colour the trolley and the objects.

3: Concepts lesson

Photocopiable worksheet *Teacher's Book page 186*

CD2 33 CD2 34 **Let's Tidy Up! song**

Messy toys, messy toys
Put them away! Put them away!
Let's tidy up now, let's tidy up now
Put the toys in the boxes now
All the toys away!

Messy clothes, messy clothes
Put them away! Put them away!
Let's tidy up now, let's tidy up now
Put the clothes in the cupboard now
All the clothes away!

- Point to the objects and say *messy* or *tidy*.
- Colour the messy objects red and the tidy objects green.
- Match the messy objects to their place.
- Sing *Let's Tidy Up!* and point to the messy and tidy objects.

Dex's values lesson

Being helpful

5 Discover my family

Name: ______________________________

4: Buddy's sounds lesson

Photocopiable worksheet *Teacher's Book page 187*

CD2 35 **Buddy's Beats rap /g/**

1, 2, 3, say with me
/g/, /g/, /g/
/g/ green!

1, 2, 3, say with me
/g/, /g/, /g/
/g/ granny!

1, 2, 3, say with me
/g/, /g/, /g/
/g/ grandad!

- Trace the letter /g/.
- Say the sound.
- Point to the pictures and say the words.
- Colour the words beginning with /g/.
- Circle the number of words you find beginning with /g/.
- Say *Buddy's Beats* and point to the words beginning with /g/.

5: Dex's values lesson: Being helpful

Pupil's Book worksheet *page 61*

- Point to the photos and say the actions and places.
- Match each action to home or school.
- Colour the frame yellow if you do the action.

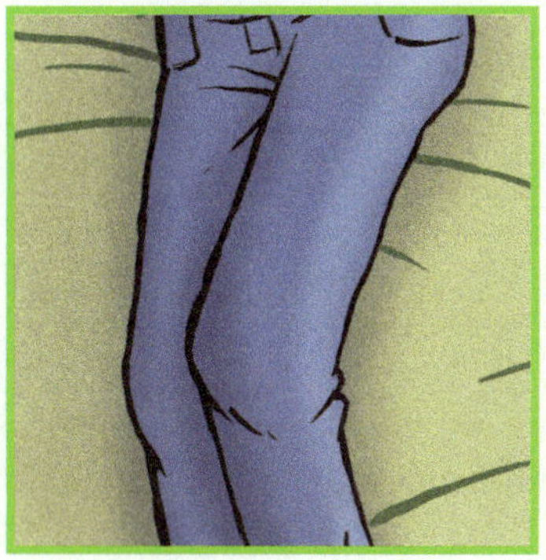

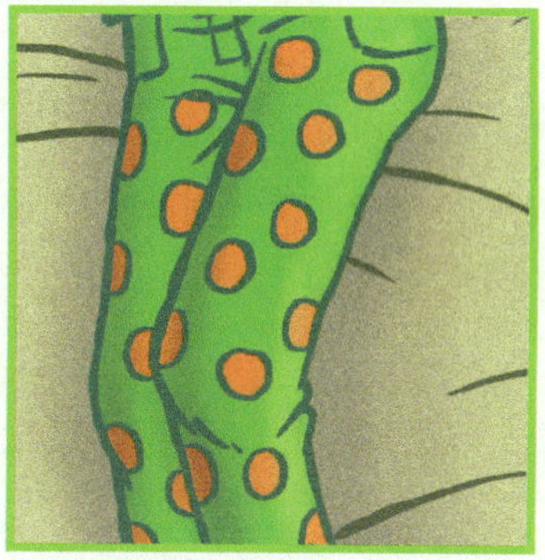

5 Discover my family

Name: ______________________

6: Kid's culture lesson

Pupil's Book worksheet *page 63*

CD2 36 CD2 37 **Diddle, Diddle, Dumpling nursery rhyme**

Diddle, diddle, dumpling, my brother John
Goes to sleep
With his trousers on
One shoe off, and one shoe on
Diddle, diddle, dumpling, my brother John!

- Point to the shapes and say the words.
- Match the correct shapes to the picture.
- Sing *Diddle, Diddle, Dumpling* and point to the picture.

7: Speaking and literacy lesson

CD2 32 **Pupil's Book worksheet (storybook)** *pages 65–66*

- Cut out and fold the pages to make the storybook.
- Listen to the story and follow the storybook with your finger.

8: Review lesson

Pupil's Book worksheet *page 67*

- Go to the sticker pages. Complete the picture with the unit stickers.
- Point to the family members and say the words.
- Stick Dex's star in the correct place.

Pupil's Book worksheet *page 68*

- Point to the pictures and say the activities.
- Draw a happy/sad face if you can/can't do the activity.

9: PLUS vocabulary lesson / Extension

Photocopiable worksheet *Teacher's Book page 188*

CD2 41 CD2 42 **My Family PLUS song**

- Point to uncle, auntie, cousin and baby, and say the words.
- Find the family members in the picture and match.
- Colour.
- Count the number of presents and circle the correct number.
- Sing *My Family PLUS* and point to the family members.

MY STORYBOOK

Name: ____________________

5

Let's Tidy Up!

Home School

5

2

1
ALADDIN
LITTLE RED RIDING HOOD
PINOCCHIO
THE WIZARD OF OZ
PETER PAN

6
PETER PAN
PINOCCHIO

3

4
DINO
BUDDY

My learning review

My progress review

Name: ______________________

I can …

Teacher: ______________________ Comments: ______________________

6 Discover food

Vocabulary lesson

6 Discover food

Name: ______________________

1: Vocabulary lesson

Pupil's Book worksheet *page 69*

CD3 2 CD3 3 **Yummy In My Tummy song**

I like soup
Yummy, yummy, yummy!
I like soup
Yum, yum, yummy!

I like vegetables
Yum, yum, yummy! (x2)
I like vegetables
Yum, yum, yummy!
Yum, yum, yummy in my tummy!

I like water
Yum, yum, yummy!
Yum, yum, yummy!
(x2)

I like meat
Yum, yum, yummy! (x2)
I like meat
Yum, yum, yummy!
Yum, yum, yummy in my tummy!

I like potatoes
Yum, yum, yummy!
Yum, yum, yummy!
(x2)

I like ice cream
Yum, yum, yummy! (x2)
I like ice cream
I like them all in my tummy!

- Point to the food and say the words.
- Complete the maze to match Meg, Charlie and Dex to the food .
- Draw yourself and your favourite food.
- Complete the maze to match yourself to your favourite food.
- Sing *Yummy In My Tummy* and point to the food.

digital ➔ **Teacher's Presentation Kit for Unit 6**

Personalisation Discover for yourself

Extra activity Draw a picture of you and your family having dinner together.

6 Discover food

Name: ______________________

2: Story lesson

Pupil's Book worksheet *page 71*

CD3 4 **I'm Hungry! story**

- Point to the food and say the words.
- Draw and colour the food Dex finds hot and cold in the story.

3: Concepts lesson

Photocopiable worksheet *Teacher's Book page 189*

CD3 5 CD3 6 **Hot And Cold song**

Can I have some hot soup, hot soup, hot soup?
Can I have some hot soup, it's cold today?
Can I have cold ice cream, ice cream, ice cream?
Can I have cold ice cream, it's hot today?

- Point to the food and say the words.
- Point to the oven and fridge and say *hot* or *cold*.
- Match the food to *hot* or *cold*.
- Colour the hot food red and the cold food blue.
- Count the number of hot and cold food items and circle the correct number for each.
- Sing *Hot And Cold* and point to the hot and cold food.

✓

✗

6 Discover food

Name: ______________________

4: Buddy's sounds lesson

Photocopiable worksheet *Teacher's Book page 190*

CD3 7 **Buddy's Beats rap /m/**

1, 2, 3, say with me
/m/, /m/, /m/
/m/ mummy!

1, 2, 3, say with me
/m/, /m/, /m/
/m/ meat!

1, 2, 3, say with me
/m/, /m/, /m/
/m/ Meg!

- Trace the letter /m/.
- Say the sound.
- Point to the pictures and say the words.
- Colour the words beginning with /m/.
- Circle the number of words you find beginning with /m/.
- Say *Buddy's Beats* and point to the words beginning with /m/.

5: Dex's values lesson: Healthy eating

Pupil's Book worksheet *page 73*

- Point to the food and say *healthy* or *not healthy*.
- Match the healthy food to the bowl with the tick.
- Match the unhealthy food to the bowl with the cross.
- Colour the bowl with the healthy food green and the bowl with the unhealthy food red.

Kid's culture lesson

1 2 3 4 5 6

1 2 3 4 5 6

6 Discover food

Name: ______________________

6: Kid's culture lesson

Pupil's Book worksheet *page 75*

CD3 8 CD3 9 **Pat A Cake nursery rhyme**

Pat a cake, pat a cake, baker man
Bake me a cake as big as you can
Mix it and mix it and mark it with 'b'
Put it in the oven for baby and me!

- Point to the cakes and say *big* or *small*.
- Find and point to the letter /b/ and say the sound.
- Count the small and big cakes and circle the correct number for each.
- Sing *Pat A Cake* and point to the picture.

7: Speaking and literacy lesson

CD3 4 **Pupil's Book worksheet (storybook)** *pages 77–78*

- Cut out and fold the pages to make the storybook.
- Listen to the story and follow the storybook with your finger.

8: Review lesson

Pupil's Book worksheet *page 79*

- Go to the sticker pages. Complete the picture with the unit stickers.
- Point to the food and say the words.
- Stick Dex's star in the correct place.

Pupil's Book worksheet *page 80*

- Point to the pictures and say the activities.
- Draw a happy/sad face if you can/can't do the activity.

9: PLUS vocabulary lesson / Extension

Photocopiable worksheet *Teacher's Book page 191*

CD3 13 CD3 14 **Yummy In My Tummy PLUS song**

- Point to the vegetables and say the words.
- Match the vegetables to the shadows.
- Colour each vegetable a different colour and say the colours.
- Sing *Yummy in My Tummy PLUS* and point to the vegetables.

MY STORYBOOK

Name: ______________________

6

I'm Hungry!

Home School

1

6
ICE CREAM

3

4

Happy Birth

My progress review

Name: ______________________________

I can ...

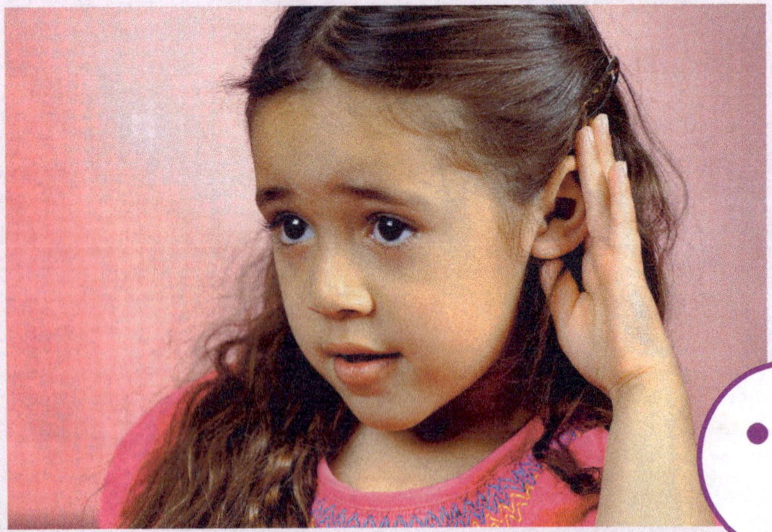

Teacher: ______________________ Comments: ______________________

7 Discover farm animals

Vocabulary lesson

1

2

3

4

1

2

3

4

7 Discover farm animals

Name: ______________________

1: Vocabulary lesson

Pupil's Book Plus worksheet *page 81*

CD3 16 CD3 17 **On The Farm song**

On the farm, on the farm
There's a chicken
Cluck, cluck, cluck (x2)
There's a chicken

On the farm, on the farm
There's a cow
Moo, moo, moo (x2)
There's a cow

On the farm, on the farm
There's a sheep
Baa, baa, baa (x2)
There's a sheep

On the farm, on the farm
There's a goat
Meeh, meeh, meeh (x2)
There's a goat

On the farm, on the farm
There's a duck
Quack, quack, quack (x2)
There's a duck

- Point to the animals and say the words.
- Match the animals to the scenes.
- Count the animals, match to the correct number and trace.
- Sing *On The Farm* and point to the animals.

digital **Teacher's Presentation Kit for Unit 7**

Personalisation Discover for yourself

Extra activity Draw your favourite farm animal.

1 2 3 4 5 6

1 2 3 4 5 6

7 Discover farm animals

Name: ______________________

2: Story lesson

Pupil's Book worksheet *page 83*

Story value

Looking after animals

CD3 18 **Where's The Missing Chick? story**

- Point to the chicks and say the word.
- Trace the numbers. Count the eggshells and circle the correct number.
- Trace the numbers. Count the chicks and circle the correct number.
- Circle the object where the missing chick was found in the story.
- Draw and colour the missing chick into the object where it was found in the story.

3: Concepts lesson

Photocopiable worksheet *Teacher's Book page 192*

CD3 19 CD3 20 **Noisy Farm, Quiet Farm song**

It's quiet, it's quiet, it's quiet
It's quiet on the farm
(x2)

It's noisy, it's noisy, it's noisy
It's noisy on the farm
(x2)

It's quiet, it's quiet, it's quiet
It's quiet on the farm
(x2)

- Point to the scene and say *noisy* or *quiet*.
- Listen to the audio and match the animals to the pictures of noisy or quiet.
- Circle the noisy animals yellow and the quiet animals blue.
- Colour the animals.
- Sing *Noisy Farm, Quiet Farm* and point to the animals.

Dex's values lesson

Looking after animals

7

Discover farm animals

Name: ______________________________

4: Buddy's sounds lesson

Photocopiable worksheet *Teacher's Book page 193*

CD3 22 **Buddy's Beats rap /d/**

1, 2, 3, say with me
/d/, /d/, /d/
/d/ daddy!

1, 2, 3, say with me
/d/, /d/, /d/
/d/ duck!

1, 2, 3, say with me
/d/, /d/, /d/
/d/ doll!

- Trace the letter /d/.
- Say the sound.
- Point to the pictures and say the words.
- Colour the words beginning with /d/.
- Circle the number of words you find beginning with /d/.
- Say *Buddy's Beats* and point to the words beginning with /d/.

5: Dex's values lesson: Looking after animals

Pupil's Book worksheet *page 85*

- Point to the photos and say whether the animal is being looked after.
- Draw a happy face if the animal is being looked after.
- Draw a sad face if the animal isn't being looked after.

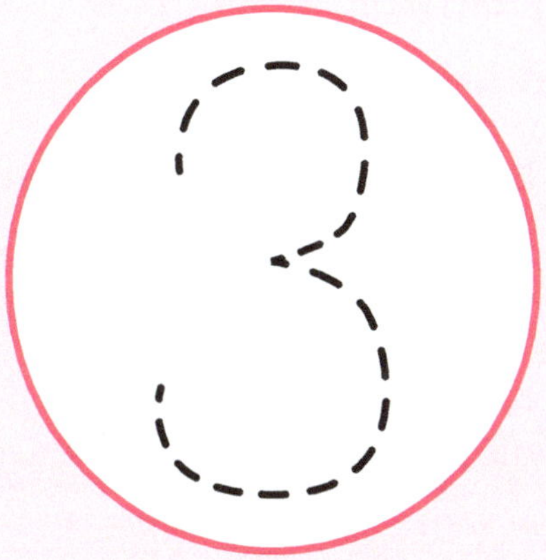

7 Discover farm animals

Name: ______________________

6: Kid's culture lesson

Pupil's Book worksheet *page 87*

CD3 23 CD3 24 **Baa Baa Black Sheep nursery rhyme**

Baa baa black sheep
Can I have some wool?
Here you are
Three bags full!

One for daddy
And one for me
And one for mummy
1, 2, 3!

- Point to the family members and say the words.
- Draw yourself in the blank frame.
- Count the number of bags of wool.
- Trace the number.
- Match a bag of wool to daddy, mummy and you.
- Colour the sheep and wool black.
- Sing *Baa Baa Black Sheep* and point to the pictures.

7: Speaking and literacy lesson

CD3 18 **Pupil's Book worksheet (storybook)** *pages 89–90*

- Cut out and fold the pages to make the storybook.
- Listen to the story and follow the storybook with your finger.

8: Review lesson

Pupil's Book worksheet *page 91*

- Go to the sticker pages. Complete the picture with the unit stickers.
- Point to the animals and say the words.
- Stick Dex's star in the correct place.

Pupil's Book worksheet *page 92*

- Point to the pictures and say the activities.
- Draw a happy/sad face if you can/can't do the activity.

9: PLUS vocabulary lesson / Extension

Photocopiable worksheet *Teacher's Book page 194*

CD3 28 CD3 29 **On The Farm PLUS song**

- Point to the animals and say the words.
- Complete the maze to match the animals.
- Colour each pair the same colour and say the colours.
- Sing *On The Farm PLUS* and point to the animals.

MY STORYBOOK

Name: ______________________

7 Where's The Missing Chick?

Home School

5

2

1

6

3

4

My progress review

Name: ______________________

I can ...

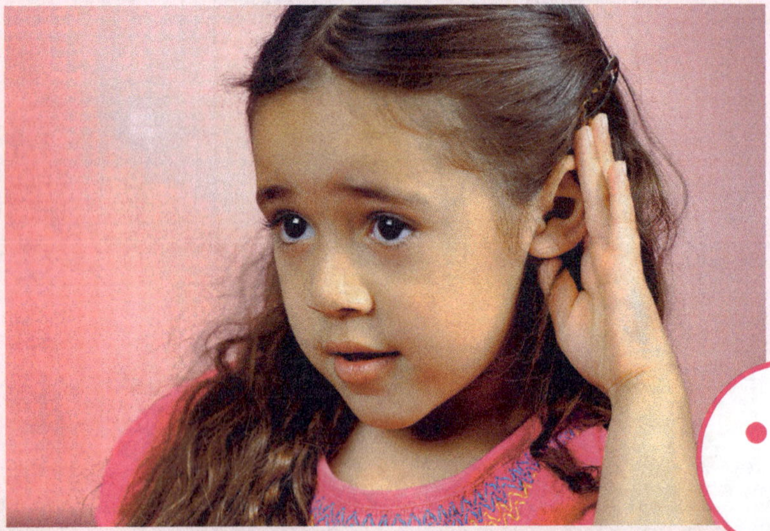

Teacher: ______________________ Comments: ______________________

8 Discover transport

Vocabulary lesson

8 Discover transport

Name: ______________________________

1: Vocabulary lesson

Pupil's Book worksheet *page 93*

CD3 31 CD3 32 **Off We Go! song**

Vroom, vroom, vroom, vroom
All in the car, all in the car!
Off we go!

Rumble, rumble, rumble, rumble
All on the bus, all on the bus!
Rumble, rumble, rumble, rumble
All on the bus, off we go!

Choo, choo, choo, choo
All on the train, all on the train!
Choo, choo, choo, choo
All on the train, off we go!

Lap, lap, lap, lap
All on the boat, all on the boat!
Lap, lap, lap, lap
All on the boat, off we go!

Whizz, whizz, whizz, whizz
Jump on your bike! Jump on your bike!
Whizz, whizz, whizz, whizz
Jump on your bike, off we go!

Zoom, zoom, zoom, zoom
All on the plane, all on the plane!
Zoom, zoom, zoom, zoom
All on the plane, off we go!

- Point to the vehicles and say the words.
- Complete the maze in the correct order.
- Sing *Off We Go!* and point to the vehicles.

digital **Teacher's Presentation Kit for Unit 8**

Personalisation Discover for yourself

Extra activity: Draw your favourite vehicle.

1 2 3 4 5 6

8 Discover transport

Name: ____________________

2: Story lesson

Pupil's Book worksheet *page 95*

CD3 33 **Let's Race! story**

- Point to the vehicles and say the words.
- Find and circle the six differences in picture 2. Say the differences.
- Trace the numbers. Count the differences and circle the correct number.
- Draw a tick for the picture that shows the story.

Six differences:
1 the bike 2 the bus 3 the boat 4 the doll
5 the ice cream 6 the clouds

3: Concepts lesson

Photocopiable worksheet *Teacher's Book page 195*

CD3 34 CD3 35 **Fast And Slow song**

Let's go fast, zoom, zoom, zoom
Let's whizz around the room!
Run fast, very fast
As fast as you can go!

Let's go slow, oh, oh, oh
Go as slow as you can go!
Walk slow, very slow
As slow as you can go!

Let's all clap very fast
Then clap very, very slow
Clap fast! Clap slow!
Well done! There you go!

- Point to the pictures and say the words.
- Point to the pictures and say *fast* or *slow*.
- Colour the fast things red and the slow things yellow.
- Draw a fast thing and a slow thing.
- Count the number of fast and slow things and trace the correct number.
- Sing *Fast And Slow* and point to the pictures.

Dex's values lesson

Taking part

8 Discover transport

Name: ____________________

4: Buddy's sounds lesson

Photocopiable worksheet *Teacher's Book page 196*

CD3 36 **Buddy's Beats rap /p/**

1, 2, 3, say with me
/p/, /p/, /p/
/p/ plane!

1, 2, 3, say with me
/p/, /p/, /p/
/p/ potatoes!

1, 2, 3, say with me
/p/, /p/, /p/
/p/ pencil!

- Trace the letter /p/.
- Say the sound.
- Point to the pictures and say the words.
- Colour the words beginning with /p/.
- Circle the number of words beginning with /p/.
- Say *Buddy's Beats* and point to the words beginning with /p/.

5: Dex's values lesson: Taking part

Pupil's Book worksheet *page 97*

- Point to the photos and say whether the photos show taking part.
- Colour the frame green if the photo shows taking part.
- Colour the frame red if the photo doesn't show taking part.
- Draw a picture of you and your friends taking part in a sport or game. Colour the frame green.

1 2 3 4 5 6

1 2 3 4 5 6

1 2 3 4 5 6

1 2 3 4 5 6

8 Discover transport

Name: ______________________

6: Kid's culture lesson

Pupil's Book worksheet *page 99*

CD3 37 CD3 38 **The Wheels On The Bus nursery rhyme**

The wheels on the bus go round and round
Round and round, round and round
The wheels on the bus go round and round
All day long!

- Point to the vehicles and say the words.
- Trace the wheels.
- Trace the numbers. Count the number of wheels on each vehicle and circle the correct number.
- Sing *The Wheels On The Bus* and point to the bus.

7: Speaking and literacy lesson

CD3 33 **Pupil's Book worksheet (storybook)** *pages 101–102*

- Cut out and fold the pages to make the storybook.
- Listen to the story and follow with your storybook.

8: Review lesson

Pupil's Book worksheet *page 103*

- Go to the sticker pages. Complete the picture with the unit stickers.
- Point to the vehicles and say the words.
- Stick Dex's star in the correct place.

Pupil's Book worksheet *page 104*

- Point to the pictures and say the activities.
- Draw a happy/sad face if you can/can't do the activity.

9: PLUS vocabulary lesson / Extension

Photocopiable worksheet *Teacher's Book page 197*

CD3 42 CD3 43 **Off We Go! PLUS song**

- Point to the vehicles and say the words.
- Trace the magnified pictures and match to the vehicles.
- Colour each vehicle a different colour and say the colours.
- Sing *Off We Go! PLUS* and point to the vehicles.

MY STORYBOOK

Name: ______________________________

8

Let's Race!

Home School

5

2

1

6

3

4

Unit 8 review lesson

My learning review

My progress review

Name: ____________________

I can …

Teacher: ____________________ Comments: ____________________

WELL DONE!
ICE CREAM

Well done!

Name: ______________________________

digital Go to the Teacher's Resource Centre for the Well Done! certificate.

Pupil's Book worksheet *page 105*

- Circle the objects from units 1–8 that you can see.
- Point to and say the objects from units 1–8 that you can see.

Personalisation Discover for yourself

Extra activity Draw your favourite character.

Discover Maths

My project 1

Measuring

My project 1

Measuring

Discover for yourself

Name: ______________________

	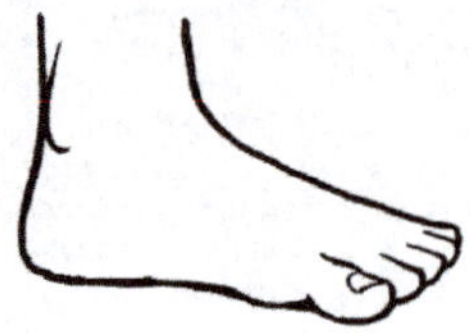	
		1 2 3 4 5 6
		1 2 3 4 5 6
		1 2 3 4 5 6

- Measure classroom objects with a paper foot.
- Draw the object and make a tally.
- Circle and say the number of feet.

Discover Art

My project 2

Patterns

Patterns

Discover for yourself

Name: ____________________

- Draw an item of clothing and make a pattern on it.

My project 3

Sounds

My project 3

Sounds

CD3 44 Discover for yourself

Name: ______________________________

- Listen to the noises.
- Colour the space red for *noisy* or green for *quiet*.

Picture dictionary Unit 1

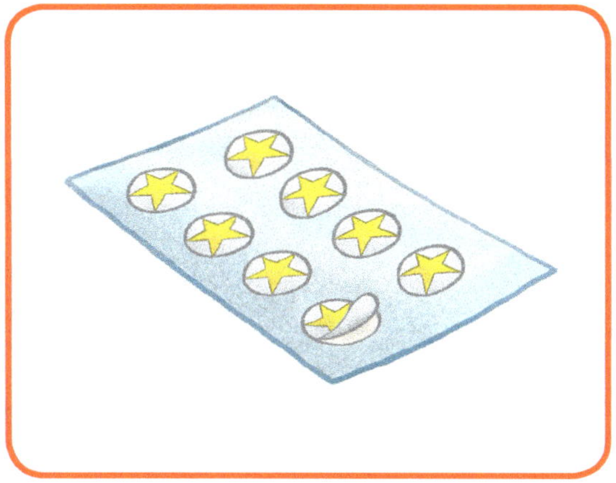

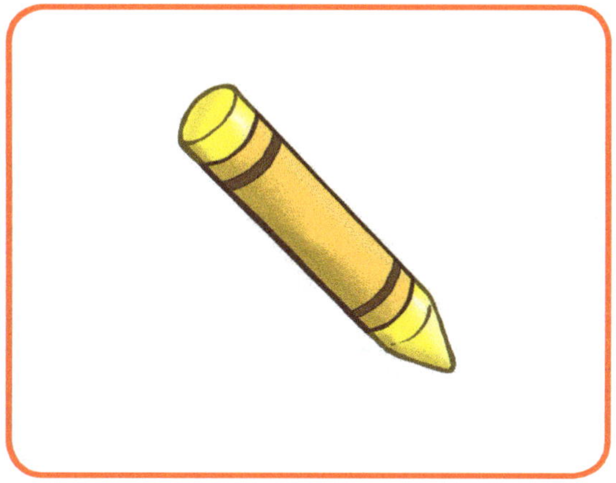

PLUS lesson ➡ *Photocopiable worksheet, Teacher's Book page 176*

Picture dictionary Unit 2

PLUS lesson ➡ *Photocopiable worksheet, Teacher's Book page 179*

Picture dictionary Unit 3

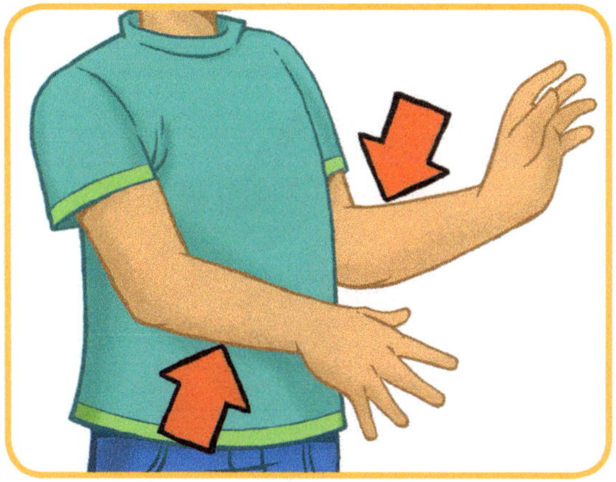

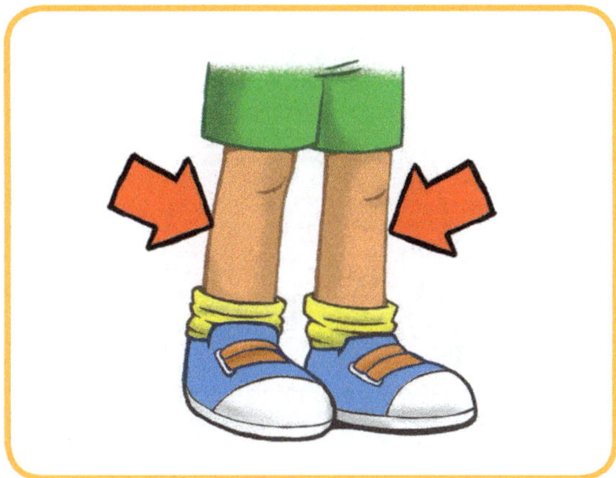
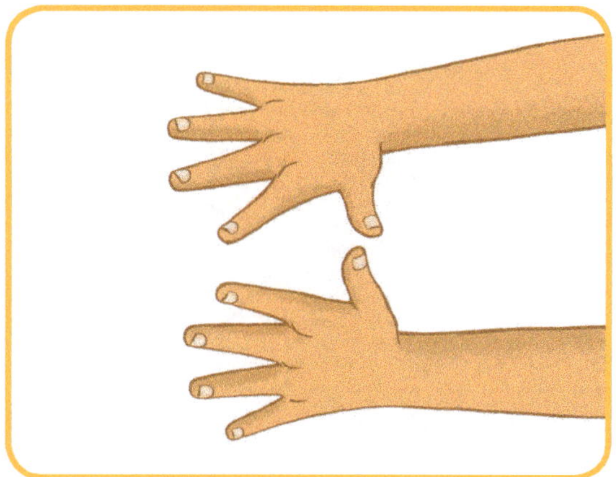
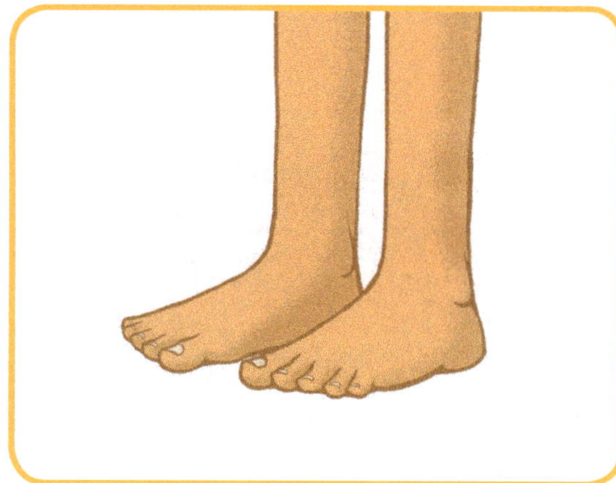

PLUS lesson ➡ *Photocopiable worksheet, Teacher's Book page 182*

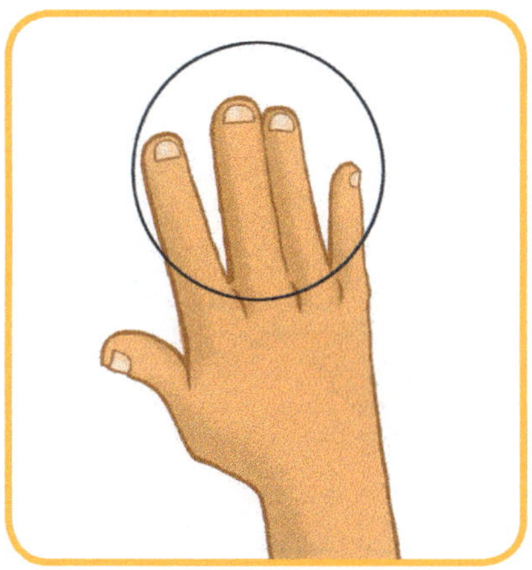
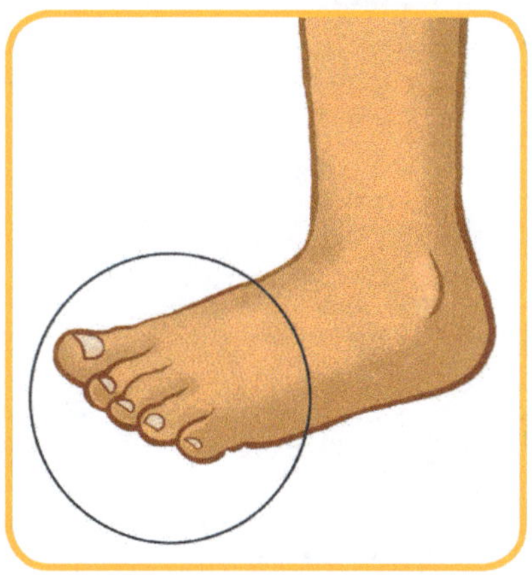

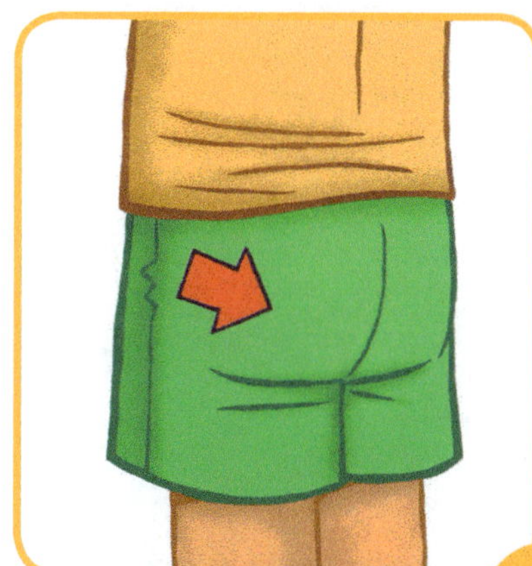

Picture dictionary Unit 4

PLUS lesson ➡ *Photocopiable worksheet, Teacher's Book page 185*

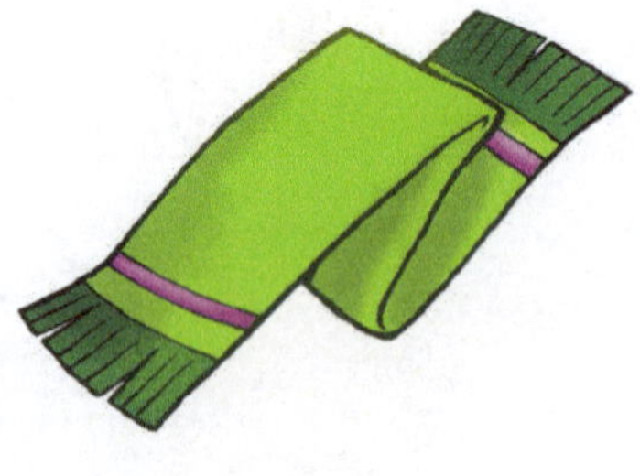

Picture dictionary Unit 5

PLUS lesson ➡ *Photocopiable worksheet, Teacher's Book page 188*

Picture dictionary Unit 6

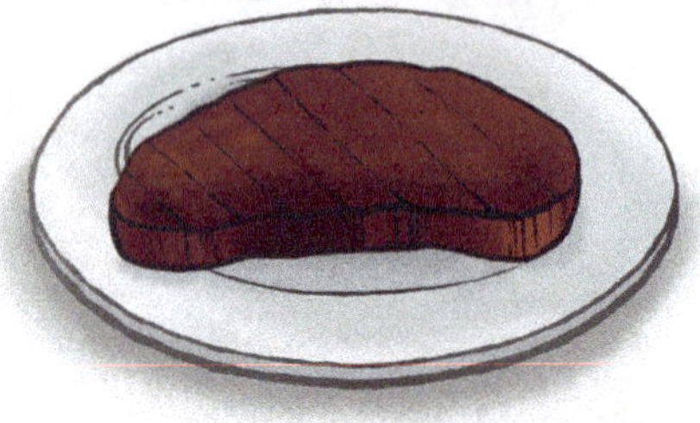

PLUS lesson ➡ *Photocopiable worksheet, Teacher's Book page 191*

Picture dictionary Unit 7

PLUS lesson ➡ *Photocopiable worksheet, Teacher's Book page 194*

Picture dictionary Unit 8

PLUS lesson ➡ *Photocopiable worksheet, Teacher's Book page 197*

Discover with Dex 1

Unit 1

Unit 2

Unit 3

Discover with Dex 1

Unit 4

Unit 5

Unit 6

Discover with Dex 1

Unit 7

Unit 8